The Rosary with Pope Francis

Compiled and with an introduction by

Marianne Lorraine Trouvé, FSP

Pauline

BOOKS & MEDIA

Boston

Cover design by Rosana Usselmann

Pope Francis photo: *L'Osservatore Romano*;
Rosary: © istockphoto.com/Arsgera

ISBN-10: 0-8198-6500-1

ISBN-13: 978-0-8198-6500-7

Published by Pauline Books & Media, 50 Saint Pauls Avenue, Boston, MA 02130–3491

Printed in the U.S.A.

www.pauline.org

Pauline Books & Media is the publishing house of the Daughters of St. Paul, an international congregation of women religious serving the Church with the communications media.

3 4 5 6 7 8 9   20 19 18 17 16

Introduction

"The Rosary is a school of prayer;
*the Rosary is a school of faith!"**

At his Sunday Angelus message on November 17, 2013, Pope Francis distributed 20,000 rosaries to the crowd, saying: "Now I would like to recommend a medicine to you. Some of you may be wondering: 'Is the Pope a pharmacist now?' It is a special medicine . . . a medicine that consists of fifty-nine threaded beads. . . . This little box contains the medicine and will be distributed to you by volunteers as you leave the Square. . . . There is a rosary, with which you can [also] pray the Chaplet of Divine Mercy, spiritual help for our souls and for spreading love, forgiveness, and brotherhood everywhere. Do not forget to take it, because it is

---

* Pope Francis, Angelus message of October 6, 2013.

good for you. It is good for the heart, the soul, and for life in general!"

In his simple way, Pope Francis tells us that the Rosary can play a very important part in our spiritual life. It is a remedy for our ills and a means to help us grow. In praying it, we think about the mysteries in the life of Jesus and Mary, and we ask for the grace to imitate their virtues.

This book contains a thought from Pope Francis for each Hail Mary. These thoughts have been culled from various homilies, addresses, and written texts of the Holy Father in which he reflects upon the mysteries in the lives of Jesus and Mary. The pope's down-to-earth way of explaining things gets right to the heart of the mysteries. The thoughts are meant to help you pray, so use them freely in whatever way you wish. You may choose to read the thought offered before each Hail Mary, or you may prefer to contemplate one or two thoughts for the entire decade or perhaps the entire Rosary. Stay with any of the reflections as long as you wish.

Although we can pray each set of mysteries on any given day, they are generally prayed on certain days of the week, as follows:

Joyful: Monday and Saturday

Luminous: Thursday

Sorrowful: Tuesday and Friday

Glorious: Wednesday and Sunday

Pope Francis has also become known for promoting a devotion to Mary, the Untier of Knots. An explanation of this devotion, along with the pope's prayer to Our Lady under this title, appears after the rosary meditations in this book (see page 88).

The Prayers of the Rosary

The Apostles' Creed

I believe in God, the Father almighty,
Creator of heaven and earth,
and in Jesus Christ, his only Son, our Lord,

(Here we bow until after the words "the Virgin Mary.")

who was conceived by the Holy Spirit,
born of the Virgin Mary,
    suffered under Pontius Pilate,
was crucified, died and was buried;
he descended into hell; on the third day he
    rose again from the dead;

he ascended into heaven, and is seated at the
right hand of God the Father almighty;
from there he will come to judge the living
and the dead.
I believe in the Holy Spirit, the holy
catholic Church,
the communion of saints, the forgiveness
of sins,
the resurrection of the body, and life
everlasting. Amen.

The Lord's Prayer

Our Father, who art in heaven, hallowed be
thy name; thy kingdom come, thy will be done
on earth as it is in heaven. Give us this day our
daily bread, and forgive us our trespasses, as we
forgive those who trespass against us, and lead
us not into temptation, but deliver us from evil.
Amen.

Hail Mary

Hail Mary, full of grace! The Lord is with
you. Blessed are you among women, and blessed
is the fruit of your womb, Jesus. Holy Mary,
Mother of God, pray for us sinners, now and at
the hour of our death. Amen.

Glory

Glory to the Father, and to the Son, and to the Holy Spirit:
as it was in the beginning, is now, and will be forever. Amen.

Hail, Holy Queen

Hail, holy Queen, Mother of mercy, our life, our sweetness, and our hope! To you we cry, poor banished children of Eve; to you we send up our sighs, mourning, and weeping in this valley of tears. Turn then, most gracious advocate, your eyes of mercy toward us, and after this our exile, show unto us the blessed fruit of your womb, Jesus. O clement, O loving, O sweet Virgin Mary.

Fatima Prayer

(Often prayed at the end of each decade of the Rosary.)

O my Jesus, forgive us our sins. Save us from the fires of hell; lead all souls into heaven, especially those in most need of your mercy. Amen.

How to Pray the Rosary

6. Pray the Hail Mary on each of the following ten beads.

18. Pray the Hail Mary on each of the following ten beads.

19. Pray the Glory after the last Hail Mary.

17. 5th Mystery Pray the Our Father.

20. End here. Pray the Hail, Holy Queen.

16. Pray the Glory after the last Hail Mary.

5. 1st Mystery and the Our Father.

7. Pray the Glory after the last Hail Mary.

15. Pray the Hail Mary on each of the following ten beads.

4. Pray the Glory.

8. 2nd Mystery Pray the Our Father.

2. Pray the Our Father.

3. Pray Hail Marys on these three beads.

9. Pray the Hail Mary on each of the following ten beads.

14. 4th Mystery Pray the Our Father.

1. Start here. Make The Sign of the Cross. Pray the Apostles' Creed.

13. Pray the Glory after the last Hail Mary.

12. Pray the Hail Mary on each of the following ten beads.

10. Pray the Glory after the last Hail Mary.

11. 3rd Mystery Pray the Our Father.

The Joyful
Mysteries

THE FIRST
JOYFUL MYSTERY

The Annunciation

Mary said, "Here am I, the servant of the Lord; let it be with me according to your word." Then the angel departed from her. (Luke 1:38, NRSV)

Our Father

Let us invoke the intercession of Mary who is the woman of the "yes." Mary said "yes" throughout her life!

Hail Mary

Mary learned to recognize Jesus's voice from the time she carried him in her womb. May Mary, our Mother, help us to know Jesus's voice better and better and to follow it, so as to walk on the path of life!

Hail Mary

The *Immaculata* was written in God's design; she is the fruit of God's love that saves the world.

Hail Mary

Our Lady never distanced herself from that love: throughout her life her whole being is a "yes" to that love, it is the "yes" to God. But that didn't make life easy for her!

Hail Mary

When the angel calls her "full of grace" (Luke 1:28), she is "greatly troubled," for in her humility she feels she is nothing before God.

Hail Mary

The angel consoles her: "Do not be afraid, Mary, for you have found favor with God. And behold, you will conceive in your womb and bear a son, and you shall call his name Jesus" (Luke 1:30, 31).

Hail Mary

This announcement troubles her even more because she was not yet married to Joseph; but the angel adds: "The Holy Spirit will come upon you . . . therefore the child to be born will be called holy, the Son of God" (Luke 1:35).

Hail Mary

Mary listens, interiorly obeys, and responds: "Behold, I am the handmaid of the Lord; let it be to me according to your word" (Luke 1:38).

Hail Mary

Let us look to her, our mother, and allow her to look upon us, for she is our mother and she loves us so much.

Hail Mary

Mary is the mother who comforts us, the mother of consolation and the mother who accompanies us on the journey.

Hail Mary

Glory be

THE SECOND
JOYFUL MYSTERY

The Visitation

And blessed is she who believed that there would be
a fulfillment of what was spoken to her by the Lord.
(Luke 1:45, NRSV)

Our Father

Mary goes to help [Elizabeth], she doesn't go to boast and tell her cousin: "Listen, I'm in charge now, because I am the Mother of God!" No, she did not do that. She went to help!

Hail Mary

Our Lady is always like this. She is our mother who always hurries to us whenever we are in need.

Hail Mary

Mary is attentive to God. She listens to God. However, Mary also listens to—that is, she interprets—the events of her life.

Hail Mary

Mary always goes in haste, she does not forget her children. And when her children are in difficulty, when they need something and call on her, she hurries to them.

Hail Mary

This is also true in our life: listening to God who speaks to us, and listening also to daily reality, paying attention to people, to events.

Hail Mary

In prayer before God who speaks, in thinking and meditating on the facts of her life, Mary is not in a hurry; she does not let herself be swept away by the moment; she does not let herself be dragged along by events.

Hail Mary

However, when she has clearly understood what God is asking of her [and] what she has to do, she does not loiter, she does not delay, but goes "with haste."

Hail Mary

Saint Ambrose commented: "There is nothing slow about the Holy Spirit."

Hail Mary

Mary, woman of listening, open our ears; grant us to know how to listen to the word of your Son Jesus among the thousands of words of this world.

Hail Mary

Mary, woman of action, obtain that our hands and feet move "with haste" toward others, to bring them the charity and love of your Son Jesus; to bring the light of the Gospel to the world, as you did.

Hail Mary

Glory be

THE THIRD
JOYFUL MYSTERY

The Birth of Jesus

For God so loved the world that he gave his only Son, so that everyone who believes in him may not perish but may have eternal life. (John 3:16, NRSV)

Our Father

[Jesus] is the Word of God who became man and pitched his "tent," his dwelling, among men.

Hail Mary

The Evangelist writes: "And the Word became flesh and dwelt among us" (John 1:14). These words, which never cease to amaze us, contain the whole of Christianity!

Hail Mary

God became mortal, fragile like us; he shared in our human condition, except for sin, but he took ours upon himself as though they were his own.

Hail Mary

He entered into our history; he became fully God-with-us!

Hail Mary

The birth of Jesus, then, shows us that God wanted to unite himself to every man and every woman—to every one of us—to communicate to us his life and his joy.

Hail Mary

Thus, Christmas reveals to us the immense love that God has for humanity. From this too derives our enthusiasm, our hope as Christians.

Hail Mary

With the birth of Jesus, a new promise is born; a new world comes into being, but also a world that can be ever renewed.

Hail Mary

However much human history and the personal story of each of us may be marked by difficulty and weakness, faith in the Incarnation tells us that God is in solidarity with humanity.

Hail Mary

The Word of God pitched his tent among us, sinners who are in need of mercy. And we all must hasten to receive the grace that he offers us.

Hail Mary

Jesus is patient, Jesus knows how to wait; he waits for us always. This is a message of hope, a message of salvation, ancient and ever new.

Hail Mary

Glory be

THE FOURTH
JOYFUL MYSTERY

The Presentation in the Temple

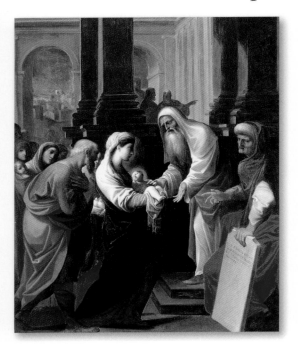

Then Simeon blessed them and said to his mother Mary, "This child is destined for the falling and the rising of many in Israel, and to be a sign that will be opposed . . . and a sword will pierce your own soul too." (Luke 2:34–35, NRSV)

Our Father

Forty days after the birth of Jesus, Mary and Joseph took the child to the Temple to offer and consecrate him to God.

Hail Mary

We are all called to offer ourselves to the Father with Jesus and like Jesus, making a generous gift of our life.

Hail Mary

This offering of self to God regards every Christian, because we are all consecrated to him in Baptism.

Hail Mary

This consecration is lived in a special way by religious, by monks and nuns . . . who by the profession of their vows belong to God in a full and exclusive way.

Hail Mary

The Feast of the Presentation of Jesus at the Temple is also . . . the encounter *between Jesus and his people*.

Hail Mary

It is a meeting *between the young and the old*: the young were Mary and Joseph with their infant son, and the old were Simeon and Anna.

Hail Mary

It is a meeting between the young, who are full of joy in observing the Law of the Lord, and the elderly who are full of joy in the action of the Holy Spirit.

Hail Mary

Jesus is at the center. It is he who moves everything, who draws all of them to the Temple, the house of his Father.

Hail Mary

Who, more than Mary, is full of the Holy Spirit? Who more than she is docile to the Spirit's action?

Hail Mary

May the grace of this mystery, the mystery of the Encounter, enlighten us and comfort us on our journey.

Hail Mary

Glory be

THE FIFTH
JOYFUL MYSTERY

The Losing and Finding of Jesus in the Temple

Then he went down with them and came to Nazareth, and was obedient to them. His mother treasured all these things in her heart. (Luke 2:51, NRSV)

Our Father

The Good Shepherd came not to be served but to serve, and to seek out and save what was lost.

Hail Mary

Draw always from Christ, the inexhaustible wellspring. . . . Advance with determination along the path of holiness; do not rest content with a mediocre Christian life.

Hail Mary

The most worthwhile thing we possess is Christ and his Gospel.

Hail Mary

The question: "Is Christ the center of my life?"
For us, for any one of us, the question "Do I truly
put Christ at the center of my life?" should not
be taken for granted.

Hail Mary

The centrality of Christ corresponds to the centrality of the Church; they are two focal points
that cannot be separated: I cannot follow Christ
except *in* the Church and *with* the Church.

Hail Mary

Apart from the Church it is not possible to find
Jesus.

Hail Mary

We have to follow Christ along the concrete path
of our daily lives so that he can transform us.

Hail Mary

Once they had returned home and were settled in Nazareth . . . Joseph instructed Jesus in his work, and Jesus learned to be a carpenter.

Hail Mary

Joseph formed little Jesus to listen to the Sacred Scriptures, above all by accompanying him on Saturday to the synagogue in Nazareth.

Hail Mary

To grow in age, to grow in wisdom, and to grow in grace: this is the work Joseph did with Jesus, to help him grow in these three ways, to aid his growth.

Hail Mary

Glory be

The Luminous
Mysteries

THE FIRST
LUMINOUS MYSTERY

The Baptism of Jesus

[John the Baptist] saw Jesus coming toward him and declared, "Here is the Lamb of God who takes away the sin of the world!" (John 1:29, NRSV)

Our Father

God's love . . . is given to us for the first time in Baptism by means of the Holy Spirit.

Hail Mary

Let us allow ourselves to be invaded by God's love! This is the great time of mercy.

Hail Mary

Jesus did not need to be baptized, but . . . with his body, with his divinity, in baptism he blessed all the waters.

Hail Mary

Before ascending to heaven, Jesus told us to go into all the world to baptize.

Hail Mary

From that day forward up until today, this has been an uninterrupted chain: they baptized their children, and their children [baptized] their own, and those children.

Hail Mary

These children are a link in a chain. You parents have a baby boy or girl to baptize, but in some years they will have a child to baptize, or a grandchild. . . . Such is the chain of faith!

Hail Mary

It is the most beautiful inheritance you will leave to [your children]: the faith.

Hail Mary

Let us ask the Holy Virgin to support us by her intercession in our commitment to follow Christ on the way of faith and charity, the path traced out by our Baptism.

Hail Mary

Let us close our eyes, let us imagine the scene on the banks of the river: John as he is baptizing and Jesus who is approaching.

Hail Mary

Let us listen to John's voice: "Behold, the Lamb of God, who takes away the sin of the world." Let us watch Jesus and in silence, each one of us, say something to Jesus from his or her heart. In silence.

Hail Mary

Glory be

THE SECOND
LUMINOUS MYSTERY

Jesus Reveals His Glory at the Wedding at Cana

When the wine gave out, the mother of Jesus said to him, "They have no wine." (John 2:3, NRSV)

Our Father

Let us trust God! Cut off from him, the wine of joy, the wine of hope, runs out. If we draw near to him, if we stay with him, what seems to be cold water, difficulty, sin, is changed into the new wine of friendship with him.

Hail Mary

We have come to knock at the door of Mary's house. She has opened it for us; she has let us in and she shows us her Son. Now she asks us to "do whatever he tells you" (John 2:5).

Hail Mary

If there is no wine, there is no feast. Can we imagine ending a wedding feast with tea or fruit juice? It doesn't work.

Hail Mary

And so our Lady asks for a miracle.... Approach [her] with joy, [be] joyful with all your heart.

Hail Mary

Naturally, there are moments of the cross, moments of sorrow, but there is always that deep sense of peace. Why? The Christian life is a feast, the wedding feast of Jesus and the Church.

Hail Mary

Jesus is the bridegroom and the Church is the bride.

Hail Mary

When you are the spouse you cannot fast, you cannot be sad. The Lord shows us that the relationship between him and the Church is matrimonial.

Hail Mary

At Mary's suggestion, in that moment Jesus reveals himself for the first time and gives a sign:

he transforms water into wine, thus saving the wedding feast.

Hail Mary

What happened in Cana 2,000 years ago happens today at every wedding celebration: that which makes your wedding full and profoundly true will be the presence of the Lord who reveals himself and gives his grace.

Hail Mary

It is the Lord's presence that offers the "good wine"; he is the secret to full joy, that which truly warms the heart.

Hail Mary

Glory be

THE THIRD
LUMINOUS MYSTERY

*Jesus Preaches the Kingdom
and Calls Us to Conversion*

"The kingdom of heaven is like treasure hidden in a field, which someone found and hid; then in his joy he goes and sells all that he has and buys that field." (Matthew 13:44, NRSV)

Our Father

God's patience has to call forth in us the courage to return to him, however many mistakes and sins there may be in our life.

Hail Mary

This is important: the courage to trust in the mercy of Jesus, to trust in his patience, to seek refuge always in the wounds of his love.

Hail Mary

Maybe someone among us here is thinking: my sin is so great, I am as far from God as the younger son in the parable; my unbelief is like that of Thomas; I don't have the courage to go back, to believe that God can welcome me and that he is waiting for me, of all people.

Hail Mary

But God is indeed waiting for you; he asks of you only the courage to go to him.

Hail Mary

How many times in my pastoral ministry have I heard it said: "Father, I have many sins"; and I have always pleaded: "Don't be afraid; go to him, he is waiting for you; he will take care of everything."

Hail Mary

For God, we are not numbers, we are important; indeed we are the most important thing to him. Even if we are sinners, we are what is closest to his heart.

Hail Mary

In the mystery of the incarnation of the Son of God there is also an aspect that is connected to human freedom, to the freedom of each one of us.

Hail Mary

We all must hasten to receive the grace that he offers us.

Hail Mary

Jesus does not desist and never ceases to offer himself and his grace, which saves us!

Hail Mary

We are called to witness with joy to this message of the Gospel of life; to the Gospel of light, of hope, and of love. For the message of Jesus is this: life, light, hope, and love.

Hail Mary

Glory be

THE FOURTH
LUMINOUS MYSTERY

The Transfiguration

Then a cloud overshadowed them, and from the cloud there came a voice, "This is my Son, the Beloved; listen to him!" (Mark 9:7, NRSV)

Our Father

We who are baptized Christians are missionary disciples, and we are called to become a living Gospel in the world.

Hail Mary

This mission of giving light to the world is so beautiful! We have this mission, and it is beautiful!

Hail Mary

It is also beautiful to keep the light we have received from Jesus, protecting it and safeguarding it.

Hail Mary

The Christian should be a luminous person; one who brings light, who always gives off light!

Hail Mary

It is truly God who gives us this light and we must give it to others. Shining lamps! This is the Christian vocation.

Hail Mary

When the Lord is transfigured before Peter, James, and John, they hear the voice of God the Father say: "This is my beloved Son! Listen to him!"

Hail Mary

The first duty of the Christian is to listen to the Word of God, to listen to Jesus, because he speaks to us and he saves us by his word.

Hail Mary

Do we take a little time each day to listen to Jesus, to listen to his word? Do we have the Gospels at home?

Hail Mary

I . . . suggest that you have a little Gospel, very little, to carry in your pocket, in your purse, and [read it] when [you] have a little time, perhaps on the bus.

Hail Mary

By his transfiguration Jesus invites us to gaze at him. And looking at Jesus purifies our eyes and prepares them for eternal life.

Hail Mary

Glory be

THE FIFTH
LUMINOUS MYSTERY

Jesus Gives Us the Eucharist

"Those who eat my flesh and drink my blood abide in me, and I in them." (John 6:56, NRSV)

Our Father

The Eucharistic Celebration is much more than a simple banquet: it is the memorial of Jesus's paschal sacrifice, the mystery at the center of salvation.

Hail Mary

Every time we celebrate this sacrament we participate in the mystery of the passion, death, and resurrection of Christ.

Hail Mary

Holy Communion conforms us in a singular and profound way to Christ.

Hail Mary

In the Eucharist, Christ is always renewing his gift of self, which he made on the cross.

Hail Mary

Does the Eucharist that I celebrate . . . urge me to go out to the poor, the sick, the marginalized?

Hail Mary

Does it help me to recognize in their [faces] the face of Jesus . . . [and] love, as Jesus wishes, those brothers and sisters who are the most needy?

Hail Mary

We go to Mass because we are sinners and we want to receive God's pardon, to participate in the redemption of Jesus, in his forgiveness.

Hail Mary

It is a gift of Christ, who makes himself present and gathers us around him, to nourish us with his word and with his life.

Hail Mary

Through the Eucharist, Christ wishes to enter into our life and permeate it with his grace, so that in every Christian community there may be coherence between liturgy and life.

Hail Mary

Let us live the Eucharist with the spirit of faith, of prayer, of forgiveness, of repentance, of communal joy, of concern for the needy . . . in the certainty that the Lord will fulfill what he has promised us: eternal life.

Hail Mary

Glory be

The Sorrowful
Mysteries

THE FIRST
SORROWFUL MYSTERY

The Agony in the Garden

In his anguish he prayed more earnestly, and his sweat became like great drops of blood falling down on the ground. (Luke 22:44, NRSV)

Our Father

On the night of Holy Thursday Jesus sweat blood. He even asked God: "Father, remove this cup from me."

Hail Mary

But, he added: "Thy will be done." And this is the difference.

Hail Mary

The Son of God offers himself to us—he puts his Body and his Blood into our hands—so as to be with us always, to dwell among us.

Hail Mary

And in the Garden of Olives, and likewise in the trial before Pilate, he puts up no resistance.

Hail Mary

He gives himself; he is the suffering Servant foretold by Isaiah, who empties himself, even unto death (see Isaiah 53:12).

Hail Mary

Jesus does not experience this love that leads to his sacrifice passively or as a fatal destiny.

Hail Mary

He does not of course conceal his deep human distress as he faces a violent death, but with absolute trust commends himself to the Father.

Hail Mary

Jesus gave himself up to death voluntarily in order to reciprocate the love of God the Father, in perfect union with his will, to demonstrate his love for us.

Hail Mary

We must all follow the path of Jesus, who himself took the road of renunciation. He became a servant, one who serves.

Hail Mary

Jesus chose to be humiliated even to the cross. And if we want to be Christians, there is no other way.

Hail Mary

Glory be

THE SECOND
SORROWFUL MYSTERY

The Scourging at the Pillar

He was wounded for our transgressions, crushed for our iniquities. (Isaiah 53:5, NRSV)

Our Father

Only the justice of God can save us! And the justice of God is revealed in the cross.

Hail Mary

The cross is the judgment of God on us all and on this world.

Hail Mary

But how does God judge us? By giving his life for us!

Hail Mary

Here is the supreme act of justice that defeated the prince of this world once and for all; and this supreme act of justice is the supreme act of mercy.

Hail Mary

Jesus calls us all to follow this path: "Be merciful, even as your Father is merciful" (Luke 6:36). I now ask of you one thing. In silence, let's all think . . . everyone think of a person with whom we are annoyed, with whom we are angry, someone we do not like.

Hail Mary

Let us think of that person and in silence, at this moment, let us pray for this person and let us become merciful with this person.

Hail Mary

The cross does not speak to us about defeat and failure; paradoxically, it speaks to us about a death which is life.

Hail Mary

The cross speaks to us of love, the love of God incarnate, a love which does not die but triumphs over evil and death.

Hail Mary

When we let the crucified Jesus gaze upon us, we are re-created, we become "a new creation."

Hail Mary

Everything else starts with this: the experience of transforming grace, the experience of being loved for no merits of our own, in spite of our being sinners.

Hail Mary

Glory be

THE THIRD
SORROWFUL MYSTERY

The Crowning with Thorns

They stripped him and put a scarlet robe on him, and after twisting some thorns into a crown, they put it on his head. (Matthew 27:28–29, NRSV)

Our Father

Let us turn to the Virgin Mary: her Immaculate Heart, a mother's heart, has fully shared in the "compassion" of God, especially in the hour of the passion and death of Jesus.

Hail Mary

May Mary help us to be mild, humble, and merciful with our brothers and sisters.

Hail Mary

The incarnate Son of God did not remove illness and suffering from human experience, but by taking them upon himself he transformed them and gave them new meaning . . .

Hail Mary

. . . [N]ew meaning because they no longer have the last word which, instead, is new and abundant life.

Hail Mary

Jesus transformed [illness and suffering], because in union with Christ they need no longer be negative but positive.

Hail Mary

Just as the Father gave us the Son out of love, and the Son gave himself to us out of the same love, so we too can love others as God has loved us.

Hail Mary

Faith in God becomes goodness; faith in the crucified Christ becomes the strength to love—even our enemies—to the end.

Hail Mary

The proof of authentic faith in Christ is self-giving and the spreading of love for our neighbors, especially for those who do not merit it, for the suffering, and for the marginalized.

Hail Mary

For us Christians, wherever the cross is, there is hope, always.

Hail Mary

The Cross of Christ invites us also to allow ourselves to be smitten by his love, teaching us always to look upon others with mercy and tenderness.

Hail Mary

Glory be

THE FOURTH
SORROWFUL MYSTERY

The Carrying of the Cross

May I never boast of anything except the cross of our Lord Jesus Christ, by which the world has been crucified to me, and I to the world. (Galatians 6:14, NRSV)

Our Father

Jesus insists on the conditions for being his disciples: preferring nothing to the love of Christ, carrying one's cross, and following him.

Hail Mary

Jesus knew well what awaited him in Jerusalem and which path the Father was asking him to take: the way of the cross.

Hail Mary

The work of Jesus is precisely a work of mercy, a work of forgiveness and love! Jesus is so full of mercy! And this universal pardon, this mercy, passes through the cross.

Hail Mary

It was his mother who was closest to him at the cross. . . . It would be good to ask her for the grace—not to take away our fear, since this must be—[but] let us ask her for the grace not to run away from the cross. She was there and she knows how to remain close to the cross.

Hail Mary

Mary is the woman whose heart was pierced by a sword and who understands all our pain.

Hail Mary

Following Jesus does not mean taking part in a triumphal procession! It means sharing his merciful love.

Hail Mary

This is the Christian's recompense and this is the path of whoever wishes to follow Jesus. For it is the path that he trod: he was persecuted.

Hail Mary

The path that Jesus trod . . . is a joyous path because the Lord never allows us to be tried beyond what we are able to bear.

Hail Mary

Let us consider: Am I ready to carry the cross like Jesus?

Hail Mary

On the cross Jesus "loved me and gave himself for me" (Galatians 2:20). Each one of us can say: "He loved me and gave himself for me." Each one can say this "for me."

Hail Mary

Glory be

THE FIFTH
SORROWFUL MYSTERY

The Crucifixion
and Death of Jesus

When Jesus saw his mother and the disciple whom he loved standing beside her, he said to his mother, "Woman, here is your son." Then he said to the disciple, "Here is your mother." (John 19:26–27, NRSV)

Our Father

On the cross . . . Jesus endured in his own flesh the dramatic encounter of the sin of the world and God's mercy.

Hail Mary

He could feel at his feet the consoling presence of his mother and his friend.

Hail Mary

At that crucial moment, before fully accomplishing the work which his Father had entrusted to him, Jesus said to Mary: "Woman, here is your son."

Hail Mary

Then he said to his beloved friend: "Here is your mother" (John 19:26–27).

Hail Mary

These words of the dying Jesus are . . . a revelatory formula which manifests the mystery of a special saving mission.

Hail Mary

Jesus left us his mother to be our mother. Only after doing so did Jesus know that "all was now finished" (John 19:28).

Hail Mary

At the foot of the cross, at the supreme hour of the new creation, Christ led us to Mary.

Hail Mary

He brought us to her because he did not want us to journey without a mother, and our people read in this maternal image all the mysteries of the Gospel.

Hail Mary

Mary, who brought him into the world with great faith, also accompanies "the rest of her offspring, those who keep the commandments of God and bear testimony to Jesus" (Revelation 12:17).

Hail Mary

Mary also experienced the martyrdom of the cross: the martyrdom of her heart, the martyrdom of her soul. She lived her Son's passion to the depths of her soul.

Hail Mary

Glory be

The Glorious
Mysteries

THE FIRST
GLORIOUS MYSTERY

The Resurrection

So if you have been raised with Christ, seek the things that are above, where Christ is, seated at the right hand of God. (Colossians 3:1, NRSV)

Our Father

Let the risen Jesus enter your life; welcome him as a friend, with trust: he is life!

Hail Mary

Christ's resurrection is not an event of the past; it contains a vital power which has permeated this world.

Hail Mary

If up until now you have kept him at a distance, step forward. He will receive you with open arms.

Hail Mary

If I let myself be touched by the grace of the Risen Christ . . . I allow the victory of Christ to be affirmed in my life, to broaden its beneficial action. This is the power of grace!

Hail Mary

With the grace of Baptism and of Eucharistic Communion I can become an instrument of God's mercy.

Hail Mary

What does it mean that Jesus is risen? It means that the love of God is stronger than evil and death itself.

Hail Mary

It means that the love of God can transform our lives and let those desert places in our hearts bloom. The love of God can do this!

Hail Mary

Jesus is risen; there is hope for you; you are no longer in the power of sin, of evil! Love has triumphed, mercy has been victorious! The mercy of God always triumphs!

Hail Mary

This is what Easter is: it is the exodus, the passage of human beings from slavery to sin and evil to the freedom of love and goodness.

Hail Mary

This is the invitation which I address to everyone: Let us accept the grace of Christ's resurrection! Let us be renewed by God's mercy.

Hail Mary

Glory be

THE SECOND
GLORIOUS MYSTERY

The Ascension

"No one has ascended into heaven except the one who descended from heaven, the Son of Man." (John 3:13, NRSV)

Our Father

During the ascension, Jesus made the priestly gesture of blessing.

Hail Mary

Jesus is the one eternal High Priest, who with his passion passed through death and the tomb and ascended into heaven.

Hail Mary

He is with God the Father, where he intercedes forever in our favor (see Hebrews 9:24).

Hail Mary

We have One who always defends us, who defends us from the snares of the devil, who defends us from ourselves and from our sins!

Hail Mary

Let us not be afraid to turn to him to ask forgiveness, to ask for a blessing, to ask for mercy!

Hail Mary

In Christ, true God and true man, our humanity was taken to God.

Hail Mary

Having seen Jesus ascending into heaven, the apostles returned to Jerusalem "with great joy."

Hail Mary

With the gaze of faith they understand that although he has been removed from their sight, Jesus stays with them for ever.

Hail Mary

The ascension does not point to Jesus's absence, but tells us that he is alive in our midst in a new way.

Hail Mary

In our life we are never alone: we have this Advocate who awaits us, who defends us.

Hail Mary

Glory be

The Third
Glorious Mystery

The Descent of the Holy Spirit

God's love has been poured into our hearts through the Holy Spirit that has been given to us. (Romans 5:5, NRSV)

Our Father

With the Holy Spirit, Mary is always present in the midst of the people.

Hail Mary

Mary joined the disciples in praying for the coming of the Holy Spirit and thus made possible the missionary outburst which took place at Pentecost.

Hail Mary

Mary is the Mother of the Church which evangelizes, and without her we could never truly understand the spirit of the new evangelization.

Hail Mary

In the Church, it is the Holy Spirit who creates harmony.

Hail Mary

Do I let myself be guided by the Holy Spirit, living in the Church and with the Church?

Hail Mary

The soul is like a sailboat; the Holy Spirit is the wind which fills its sails and drives it forward, and the gusts of wind are the gifts of the Spirit.

Hail Mary

The Holy Spirit draws us into the mystery of the living God and saves us from the threat of a Church that is . . . closed in on herself.

Hail Mary

The Holy Spirit is the soul of *mission*.

Hail Mary

The Holy Spirit is the supreme gift of the risen Christ to his apostles, yet he wants that gift to reach everyone.

Hail Mary

The Paraclete Spirit, the "Comforter," grants us the courage to take to the streets of the world, bringing the Gospel!

Hail Mary

Glory be

THE FOURTH
GLORIOUS MYSTERY

The Assumption

A great portent appeared in heaven: a woman clothed with the sun, with the moon under her feet, and on her head a crown of twelve stars. (Revelation 12:1, NRSV)

Our Father

Let us entrust our praise to the hands of the Virgin Mary.

Hail Mary

She, the most humble of creatures, thanks to Christ has already arrived at the destination of the earthly pilgrimage: she is already in the glory of the Trinity.

Hail Mary

For this reason Mary our Mother, our Lady, shines out for us as a sign of sure hope.

Hail Mary

She is also the mother who comforts us, the mother of consolation and the mother who accompanies us on the journey.

Hail Mary

In the struggle which . . . all of us, all the disciples of Jesus, must face, Mary does not leave us alone.

Hail Mary

The Mother of Christ and of the Church is always with us. She walks with us always, she is with us.

Hail Mary

Mary accompanies us, struggles with us, sustains Christians in their fight against the forces of evil.

Hail Mary

Prayer with Mary, especially the Rosary, has this "suffering" dimension, that is of struggle, a sustaining prayer in the battle against the Evil One and his accomplices.

Hail Mary

The Rosary also sustains us in the battle.

Hail Mary

Christ is the first fruits from the dead and Mary is the first of the redeemed, the first of "those who are in Christ."

Hail Mary

Glory be

THE FIFTH
GLORIOUS MYSTERY

Mary Is Crowned Queen
of Heaven and Earth

"Be faithful until death, and I will give you the crown of life." (Revelation 2:10, NRSV)

Our Father

When you express profound devotion for the Virgin Mary, you are pointing to the highest realization of the Christian life.

Hail Mary

By her faith and obedience to God's will, and by her meditation on the words and deeds of Jesus, Mary is the Lord's perfect disciple.

Hail Mary

Let us ask the Virgin Mary to teach us to encounter one another in Jesus every day.

Hail Mary

Watch over me, Mother, when I am disoriented, and lead me by the hand.

Hail Mary

May you spur us on to meet our many brothers and sisters who are on the outskirts, who are hungry for God but have no one to proclaim him.

Hail Mary

May Mary, the Mother of God and our tender Mother, support us always, that we may remain faithful to our Christian vocation.

Hail Mary

Mary prays, she prays together with the community of the disciples, and she teaches us to have complete trust in God and in his mercy. This is the power of prayer!

Hail Mary

Let us never tire of knocking at God's door.
Every day through Mary let us carry our entire
life to God's heart! Knock at the door of God's
heart!

Hail Mary

We need Mary's tender gaze; her maternal gaze,
which knows us better than anyone else; her
gaze full of compassion and care.

Hail Mary

Mother, grant us your gaze! Your gaze leads us
to God; your gaze is a gift of the good Father
who waits for us at every turn of our path.

Hail Mary

Glory be

Devotion to Mary, Untier of Knots

This devotion, although not well-known, is becoming more popular because Pope Francis has been promoting it. When he was a Jesuit priest studying in Germany, Father Jorge Mario Bergoglio came across a beautiful painting of Mary that impressed him deeply. The painting portrays an angel giving Mary a long cord full of knots. Patiently the Virgin is undoing the knots and straightening out the cord. This symbolism reflects a deeper spiritual reality: that Mary's intercession can help us untangle the various complicated situations we weave in our lives.

The devotion is actually based on a long-standing comparison of Mary with Eve. Saint Irenaeus, an early Church Father, wrote during the second century, "The knot of Eve's disobedience was loosed by the obedience of Mary. For what the virgin Eve had bound fast through unbelief, this did the virgin Mary set free through faith" (*Adversus Haereses*, 3, 22). Pope Francis further comments, "Even the most tangled knots are loosened by his grace. And Mary, whose 'yes' opened the door for God to undo the knot of the ancient disobedience, is the mother who patiently and lovingly brings us to God, so that he can untangle the knots of our souls by his fatherly mercy" (*Marian Prayer for the Year of Faith*, October 12, 2013).

Pope Francis wrote the following prayer to Our Lady Untier of Knots, which can be prayed as a novena (a prayer or set of prayers repeated for nine days) or whenever desired:

> Holy Mary, full of God's presence during
>   the days of your life,
> you accepted with full humility the Father's
>   will,
> and the Devil was never able to tie you
>   around with his confusion.
> Once with your Son you interceded for our
>   difficulties,

and, full of kindness and patience you gave
   us an example of how to untie the
   knots of our life.
By remaining forever our Mother,
you put in order, and make more clear the
   ties that link us to the Lord.
Holy Mother, Mother of God and our
   Mother,
who untie with a motherly heart the knots
   of our life, we pray to you to receive in
   your hands (*the name of a person*),
and to free him/her of the knots and confu-
   sion with which our enemy attacks.
Through your grace, your intercession, and
   your example,
deliver us from all evil, our Lady, and untie
   the knots that prevent us from being
   united with God,
so that we, free from sin and error, may find
   him in all things, may have our hearts
   placed in him, and may serve him
   always in our brothers and sisters.
   Amen.

Prayers to Mary
by Pope Francis

Mary, woman of listening, open our ears; grant us to know how to listen to the word of your Son Jesus among the thousands of words of this world; grant that we may listen to the reality in which we live, to every person we encounter, especially those who are poor, in need, in hardship.

Mary, woman of decision, illuminate our mind and our heart, so that we may obey, unhesitatingly, the word of your Son Jesus; give us the courage to decide, not to let ourselves be dragged along, letting others direct our life.

Mary, woman of action, obtain that our hands and feet move "with haste" toward others, to bring them the charity and love of your Son,

Jesus, to bring the light of the Gospel to the world, as you did. Amen.

— *May 31, 2013, conclusion of the Marian Month of May*

Mother, help our faith!

Open our ears to hear God's word and to recognize his voice and call.

Awaken in us a desire to follow in his footsteps, to go forth from our own land and to receive his promise.

Help us to be touched by his love, that we may touch him in faith.

Help us to entrust ourselves fully to him and to believe in his love, especially at times of trial, beneath the shadow of the cross, when our faith is called to mature.

Sow in our faith the joy of the Risen One.

Remind us that those who believe are never alone.

Teach us to see all things with the eyes of Jesus, that he may be light for our path. And may this light of faith always increase in us, until the dawn of that undying day which is Christ himself, your Son, our Lord!

— *At the conclusion of the encyclical* Lumen Fidei

Acknowledgments

SOURCES

Excerpts from Pope Francis's audiences, homilies, angelus messages, addresses, messages and exhortations copyright © Libreria Editrice Vaticana. Used with permission.

Unless otherwise noted, the Scripture quotations contained herein are taken directly from Pope Francis's works.

All other Scripture quotations contained herein are from the *New Revised Standard Version Bible: Catholic Edition,* copyright © 1989, 1993, Division of Christian Education of the National Council of the Churches of Christ in the United States of America. Used by permission. All rights reserved.

The English translation of the Apostles' Creed from *The Roman Missal* © 2010, International Commission on English in the Liturgy Corporation. All rights reserved.

English translation of Glory by the International Consultation on English Texts (ICET).

The English translation of Pope Francis's prayer: To Mary, Untier of Knots, copyright © Libreria Editrice Vaticana. Used with permission.

Pope Francis photo: © *L'Osservatore Romano* photo service.

Joyful Mysteries

The Annunciation

1–3	Regina Caeli, April 21, 2013
4–9	Angelus, December 8, 2013
10	Angelus, May 26, 2013

The Visitation

1–2	Homily, May 26, 2013
3	Address, May 31, 2013
4	Homily, May 26, 2013
5–10	Address, May 31, 2013

The Birth of Jesus

1–10	Angelus, January 5, 2014

The Presentation in the Temple

1–4	Angelus, February 2, 2014
5–10	Homily, February 2, 2014

The Losing and Finding of Jesus in the Temple

1	Homily, April 21, 2013
2	Homily, May 5, 2013
3	Homily, May 12, 2013
4–5	Homily, July 31, 2013
6	Homily, April 23, 2013
7	Homily, May 5, 2013
8–10	General audience, March 19, 2014

Luminous Mysteries

The Baptism of Jesus

Jesus Reveals His Glory at the Wedding at Cana

Jesus Preaches the Kingdom and Calls Us to Conversion

The Transfiguration

Jesus Gives Us the Eucharist

Sorrowful Mysteries

The Agony in the Garden

The Scourging at the Pillar

The Crowning with Thorns

The Carrying of the Cross

The Crucifixion and Death of Jesus

Glorious Mysteries

The Resurrection

The Ascension

The Descent of the Holy Spirit

The Assumption

Mary Is Crowned Queen of Heaven and Earth

ART SOURCES

Joyful Mysteries

Annunciation

Carl Heinrich Bloch. *The Annunciation* (ca. before 1890). Chapel at Frederiksborg Palace, Copenhagen. http://commons.wikimedia.org/wiki/File:Carl_Heinrich_Bloch_-_The_Annunciation.jpg.

Visitation

Raphael Sanzio, Giulio Romano, and Giovan Francesco Penni. *The Visitation* (*La Visitación*) (ca. 1517). Museum of Prado, Madrid. http://commons.wikimedia.org/wiki/File%3ARaphael_-_The_visitation.jpg.

Nativity

Jean-Baptiste Marie Pierre. *The Nativity* (second half of 18th century). Private collection. http://commons.wikimedia.org/wiki/File%3AJean-Baptiste_Marie_Pierre_-_Nativity_-_WGA17676.jpg.

Presentation

Ludovico Carracci. *The Presentation of the Christ Child in the Temple* (ca. 1605). Thyssen-Bornemisza Museum, Madrid. http://commons.wikimedia.org/wiki/File%3ALodovico_Carracci_-_Presentation_in_the_Temple_-_WGA4472.jpg.

Finding of Jesus in the Temple

Ludovico Mazzolino. *The Twelve-Year-Old Jesus Teaching in the Temple* (ca. 1524). Gemäldegalerie, Berlin. http://commons.wikimedia.org/wiki/File%3ALodovico_Mazzolino_-_The_Twelve-Year-Old_Jesus_Teaching_in_the_Temple_-_Google_Art_Project.jpg.

LUMINOUS MYSTERIES

Baptism of Jesus

Guido Reni. *The Baptism of Christ* (ca. 1623). Kunsthistorisches Museum Wien, Gemèldegalerie, Vienna. http://commons.wikimedia.org/wiki/File%3AGuido_Reni_063.jpg.

Wedding Feast at Cana

Julius Schnorr von Carolsfeld. *The Wedding Feast at Cana* (1819). Kunsthalle, Hamburg. http://commons.wikimedia.org/wiki/File%3AJulius_Schnorr_von_Carolsfeld_-_The_Wedding_Feast_at_Cana_-_WGA21013.jpg.

Jesus Announces the Kingdom

Carl Heinrich Bloch. *The Sermon on the Mount* (1871/1877). The Museum of National History at Frederiksborg Castle, Hillerød. http://commons.wikimedia.org/wiki/File%3ABloch-SermonOnTheMount.jpg.

The Transfiguration

Carl Heinrich Bloch. *The Transfiguration* (1872). The Museum of National History at Frederiksborg Castle, Hillerød. http://commons.wikimedia.org/wiki/File%3ATransfiguration_bloch.jpg.

The Eucharist

Jacopo Tintoretto. Detail, *The Last Supper* (between 1592 and 1594). San Giorgio Maggiore, Venice. http://commons.wikimedia.org/wiki/File%3AJacopo_Tintoretto_-_The_Last_Supper_(detail)_-_WGA22563.jpg.

Sorrowful Mysteries

Agony in the Garden

José Claudio Antolinez. *Prayer in the Garden of Olives* (Oración en el huerto de los Olivos) (1665). Bowes Museum, Bernard Castle, U.K. http://commons.wikimedia.org/wiki/File%3AAntolinez-huerto_olivos-bowes.jpg.

Scourging at the Pillar

Michael Pacher. *Flagellation of Christ* (between 1495 and 1498). Österreichische Galerie Belvedere, Vienna. http://commons.wikimedia.org/wiki/File:Michael_Pacher_-_Flagellation_-_WGA16816.jpg.

Crowning with Thorns

Hendrick ter Brugghen. *Crowning with Thorns* (ca. 1614). Museum of John Paul II Collection, Porczyński Gallery, Warsaw. http://commons.wikimedia.org/wiki/File%3ABrugghen_Crowning_with_Thorns.JPG.

Carrying of the Cross

Giovanni Bellini or possibly Vincenzo Catena. Close up of *Christ Carrying the Cross* (between 1505 and 1510). Isabella Stewart Gardner Museum, Boston. http://commons.wikimedia.org/wiki/File%3ACircle_of_Giovanni_Bellini_-_Christ_carrying_the_cross.jpg.

Crucifixion

Carl Heinrich Bloch. *Christ on the Cross* (1870). The Museum of National History at Frederiksborg Castle, Hillerød. http://commons.wikimedia.org/wiki/File%3AChrist_at_the_Cross_-_Cristo_en_la_Cruz.jpg.

GLORIOUS MYSTERIES

Resurrection

Peter Paul Rubens. *Christ Risen* (ca. 1616). Palazzo Pitti, Florence. http://commons.wikimedia.org/wiki/File%3APeter_Paul_Rubens_-_Christ_Resurrected_-_WGA20203.jpg.

Ascension

Benvenuto Tisi da Garofalo. *Ascension of Christ* (between 1510 and 1520). Galleria Nazionale d'Arte Antica, Rome. http://commons.wikimedia.org/wiki/File%3ABenvenuto_Tisi_da_Garofalo_-_Ascension_of_Christ_-_WGA08474.jpg.

Descent of the Holy Spirit

Jean Restout II. *Pentecost* (1732). Louvre Museum, Paris. http://commons.wikimedia.org/wiki/File%3AJean_II_Restout_-_Pentecost_-_WGA19318.jpg.

Assumption

Guido Reni. *The Assumption of (the Virgin) Mary* (1627). Church of Mary of the Assumption, Castelfranco, Emilia. http://commons.wikimedia.org/wiki/File%3AAssunzione_di_Maria.jpg.

Coronation

Paolo Veronese Caliari. *Coronation of the Virgin* (1555). Church of San Sebastiano, Venice. http://commons.wikimedia.org/wiki/File%3APaolo_Veronese_-_Coronation_of_the_Virgin_-_WGA24795.jpg.

BOOKS & MEDIA

The Daughters of St. Paul operate book and media centers at the following addresses. Visit, call, or write the one nearest you today, or find us at www.pauline.org.

CALIFORNIA
3908 Sepulveda Blvd, Culver City, CA 90230   310-397-8676
935 Brewster Avenue, Redwood City, CA 94063   650-369-4230

FLORIDA
145 S.W. 107th Avenue, Miami, FL 33174   305-559-6715

HAWAII
1143 Bishop Street, Honolulu, HI 96813   808-521-2731

ILLINOIS
172 North Michigan Avenue, Chicago, IL 60601   312-346-4228

LOUISIANA
4403 Veterans Memorial Blvd, Metairie, LA 70006   504-887-7631

MASSACHUSETTS
885 Providence Hwy, Dedham, MA 02026   781-326-5385

MISSOURI
9804 Watson Road, St. Louis, MO 63126   314-965-3512

NEW YORK
64 W. 38th Street, New York, NY 10018   212-754-1110

SOUTH CAROLINA
243 King Street, Charleston, SC 29401   843-577-0175

TEXAS
Currently no book center; for parish exhibits or outreach evangelization, contact: 210-569-0500, or SanAntonio@paulinemedia.com, or P.O. Box 761416, San Antonio, TX 78245

VIRGINIA
1025 King Street, Alexandria, VA 22314   703-549-3806

CANADA
3022 Dufferin Street, Toronto, ON M6B 3T5   416-781-9131